The Sea Lion

Ocean Diver

text by Joëlle Pichon
photos by Sophie and Patrick de Wilde

 Charlesbridge

Library of Congress Cataloging-in-Publication Data
Pichon, Joëlle.
    [otarie, espiègle sirène. English]
    The sea lion: ocean diver/text by Joëlle Pichon; photographs
by Sophie and Patrick de Wilde.
        p.   cm. — (Animal close-ups)
    Summary: Examines the physical characteristics and habits of
the sea lion.
    ISBN 0-88106-438-6 (softcover)
    1. Sea lions—Juvenile literature. [1. Sea lions.] I. Wilde,
Sophie de, ill. II. Wilde, Patrick de, ill. III. Title. IV. Series.
QL737.P63P5313 1997   96-17855
599.74'6—dc20

Photographs copyright © 1992 by Sophie and Patrick de Wilde: covers,
pp. 3-23, p. 24 (top), pp. 25-27
Copyright © 1992 by Éditions Milan under the title *l'otarie, espiègle sirène*
300, rue Léon-Joulin, 31101 Toulouse Cedex 100, France
French series editor, Valérie Tracqui
Translated by Boston Language Institute

The male sea lion is impressive. He can weigh more than five hundred pounds.

Tropical paradise

A long time ago, near the equator, mountains of black lava rose out of the blue waters of the Pacific Ocean. Tropical breezes carried seeds that planted these small volcanic islands with rare cacti and trees. Powerful currents and waves carved out the landscape of caves, lagoons, and sandy inlets of the Galapagos archipelago.

These islands belong to brown pelicans, albatross, red crabs, and sea iguanas. They are ruled by the eared seal, the sea lion of the Galapagos Islands.

A small volcano towers over a beach of white sand and volcanic rock. The Galapagos Islands are a paradise for sea lions.

The life of a bull

Spring arrives in the Galapagos Islands. For the sea lions, this is the season for change and romance. A large bull has conquered his territory after a hard fight. He is now in charge of a sandy beach and part of the seashore, and he will defend them jealously against his rivals.

About thirty female sea lions, or cows, and their pups make up his new colony. Many of the cows are pregnant and getting ready to give birth. This bull will care for the females and their offspring even though he is not necessarily the father of all of the babies. The cows will obey this bull as long as they live in his territory, but they may leave whenever they wish.

All day long, the bull swims close to the shore. He grunts to invite his companion to join him.

When the bull is defending his territory, he is so busy he forgets to eat. This can last for several weeks.

The male is much bigger than the female and has a large bump on his forehead.

A baby seal weighs about ten pounds at birth. It is hungry and grows quickly, thanks to its mother's rich milk.

While mom is napping, this pup takes a look around.

On a beach of red sand, a mother rests with her baby.

A cow tickles her pup with her whiskers as they get to know each other.

If its mother disappears, a young orphan will not be able to survive. None of the other females will care for it.

An attentive mother

One cow slips away from the colony. She is pregnant, and it is hard for her to move on the shore. On the sand, in the shade of a bush, her pup comes into the world headfirst.

The mother licks her baby gently and sniffs it, absorbing its scent so she will never forget it. The pup, who is already hungry, bleats for the first time. The mother's flipper guides the baby to her teats, and the pup begins to feed.

The pair get to know each other between sunbaths and washing sessions. Only after this period of bonding will the mother introduce her baby to the whole herd.

Childhood games

Within a colony of sea lions, all births take place at about the same time. When the babies are about one month old, their mothers leave to go fishing. The young pups are gathered together and supervised by another adult female. They create an uproar on the beach and splash noisily in the natural pools, but they do not leave the shore.

Shortly after the birth of the pups, the bull will mate with many of the mothers to make sure that the cycle of births will continue the next year. The bull protects the members of his colony. If a shark approaches, he warns the others, and he will risk his own life to chase away the enemy.

In the heat of the islands, it is fun to splash around in a pool.

10

Sea lion pups love to play.

A young pup curls up for a nap.

At first the young sea lion is afraid of the waves. His mother will teach him to dive while she plays with him.

"Sea lion"

People have nicknamed the eared seal the "sea lion" because of the male's roar. In some species, the males also have fur around their necks, just like a lion's mane. Like other seals, the eared seal is an amphibious mammal. Although it spends most of its life in the water, it also loves to sunbathe on the shore.

The sea lion has small, cone-shaped ears, which makes it different from its cousins, the earless seals. Earless seals drag themselves around on land like caterpillars, but eared seals use their four limbs like levers to move about on the sand or to climb rocks.

In a deep dive the sea lion's lungs, filled with air, can resist very high pressures.

The sea lion is never cold. Its blubber and coat keep it warm and are great for diving. Its coat, which is black and shiny when wet, turns golden as it dries in the sun.

A school of fish swims in front of a hungry sea lion.

When it is about five months old, the young sea lion begins to fish on its own.

Fishing

Between naps on the hot sand, a sea lion yawns. Her pup is asleep next to her, finally satisfied after a long feeding. This mother is hungry, and hot from the sun. It is time for her to cool off and eat, so she leaves the beach and slides into the waves for a quick dive.

The Galapagos sea lion fishes during the day. As soon as it finds a school of fish, all of its senses become alert. Its mustache quivers and its eyes widen. It scares herring or sardines as it spins and twirls in the water. Sea lions are always hungry and will even eat shellfish and small squid.

Like many other carnivores, the sea lion has very sharp teeth.

The sea lion seems to fly through the blue water.

A gray shark lies in wait.

Ocean diver

Little is known about the life of the sea lion in deep water, but it is remarkably well adapted to diving. It can dive more than six hundred feet and can hold its breath for as long as ten minutes. Its nostrils and throat close by reflex, so it can swallow its prey without getting a mouthful of water or risking drowning.

For the sea lion, the ocean is a place for games. But it can also be dangerous. In the Galapagos Islands, sharks are the sea lions' enemy. When a careless sea lion returns from a dive or swims around a rock, it can be caught in a shark's sharp jaws.

Riding the waves

The sea lion of the Galapagos Islands takes advantage of its island paradise. It is sociable, sweet, and playful, but it can also be aggressive.

On the shore, it warms itself, sleeping and sunbathing. Curious, it will play with anything. A favorite toy might be a sea urchin or a piece of seaweed.

On land, sea lions are as clumsy as puppies. In the water, they act like clowns. Their favorite sport is surfing, and they are skilled at riding the waves. They float on their backs and swim out into the sea, waiting for the roll of foam that will carry them back to shore.

A starfish makes a great toy.

In the waves, the Galapagos sea lion is a champion surfer.

Time to wash up!

Sea lions love to float.

19

A lazy young sea lion shares its rock with red crabs, a sea iguana, and unusual birds: blue-footed boobies.

The school of life

The young sea lions are now between six and seven months old. Thanks to their mothers' rich milk, they weigh about fifty pounds. They are becoming more independent, and they follow the adults in their fishing parties.

The young females, small and graceful, rarely leave their mothers. The young males are already acting competitive. With their chests thrown out, they test their strength in play fighting that prepares them to become adult bulls.

The mothers sometimes allow their pups from the preceding year to nurse along with their new babies.

Two young bulls confront each other in a test of strength.

Time to rest

Calm slowly returns to the colony. The bull is thin and exhausted from defending his territory and from breeding. He needs a rest from outside threats and from the other bulls who have tried to take over his position. In the peace of a rocky inlet or a lagoon, he regains his health. It is a new year in the life cycle of the colony, and the bull must soon fight for his territory again.

The tired bull takes a vacation with the flamingos in a peaceful lagoon.

For some sea lions, it is once again the season for a change. They swim away looking for new islands and shores to explore.

This female is not tempted by adventure. She has decided to remain part of this colony.

For some of the cows, the call of the ocean is strong, and they feel it is time to move on. They leave, accompanied by the pups that they will nurse for another year. Many of these mothers are pregnant again, and they will give birth when they are settled in their new colonies.

Fishermen's prey

The sea lions, or eared seals, like their cousins the earless seals, have always been hunted by humans. For centuries their coats, blubber, and meat were the main resources some people had for survival. Today, in many parts of the world, fishermen are declaring war on sea lions because they think they eat too many fish. In other regions, the bulls are hunted to be sold in Asia, where their bones are thought to have magical powers.

Clowning around

The eared seal of the Galapagos Islands is a subspecies of the California sea lion, the most playful of the seal family. Their pretty faces and skill in the water make them a favorite with trainers. They can often be found balancing balls on their noses in circus rings or playing the clown in aquariums.

An audience enjoys this seal's performance.

Drifting nets

In recent years, as ocean resources have been exhausted, a ruthless fishing technique has been used to capture more and more tuna. Nylon nets that can be more than forty miles long are used to trap everything in their path. They catch fish, but they also capture dolphins, sea tortoises, whales, sharks, and seals.

In the port of Santa Barbara, California, a seal is resting on a dock.

A wounded female waits for someone to remove pieces of a nylon trap from her neck.

Care centers

This fishing is cruel, especially for marine species without commercial value. In many places, governments have now restricted the use of these nets, which has helped reduce this blind massacre. In California, some nature protectors have opened centers where they collect wounded seals on the beaches and care for them until they can be released.

A young seal, on the path to recovery, eats a last meal before being set free.

The world of seals

There are fourteen different species of eared seals. They swim in all the oceans of the world, from the coldest to the warmest. Five of these species are considered sea lions and nine of them are fur seals. Like their cousins, the earless seals and walruses, sea lions have powerful flippers. Adult sea lions have thin coats and snouts that are almost round. Fur seals have pointed noses, like mice, and coats of thick hair or fur.

▲
The *Antarctic fur seal* lives in small colonies on some windy islands close to the South Pole. It feeds on squid, fish, and small shrimp that it catches in the frozen waters. Its fur is silvery, and the adults have long hairs on their heads that bristle as a sign of aggression.

▲
The *South American sea lion* lives on the Atlantic and Pacific coasts of South America. The cow seems tiny next to the bull, which is nicknamed "the maned sea lion." The largest of the males can be close to ten feet long and can weigh more than seven hundred pounds.

◄ The *New Zealand fur seal* lives only in New Zealand and Australia. Like many members of its species, it is a rock climber. It is easy to recognize by its pointed snout and the golden hairs scattered throughout its dark coat.

The *South American fur seal* is found most frequently on the rocky islands along the Atlantic and Pacific coasts of South America. It is rare to see colonies on the mainland, except in Peru.

▼

The *Australian sea lion* lives in the warm waters that border the west and south sides of this continent. Members of this family are often eaten by great white sharks. The females can be recognized by their coats, which are white on their chests and stomachs and dark gray on their backs.

Hooker's sea lion makes its home in New Zealand. The adults spend most of the year in the sea and return to land in December to reproduce. The bull defends a very small territory around him. This species has long been hunted for its fur, but today it is protected.

▶

27

For Further Reading . . .

A First Look at Seals, Sea Lions, and Walruses. Millicent Ellis Selsam. Illustrated by Harriet Springer. Walker and Co., 1988.

Sea Lion. Caroline Arnold. Photographs by Richard Hewett. William Morrow, 1994.

Seals & Sea Lions : An Affectionate Portrait. Vicki Leon. Illustrated by Frank Balthis. Silver Burdett, 1994.

Use the Internet to Find Out More . . .

Yahooligans **http://www.yahooligans.com/Science_and_Oddities/Animals/**
      Sea lion information is scattered but this is a good place to start.

Sea Lion Information **http://elpc54136.lut.ac.uk/sealions.html**
      This personal site lists a few places to find information.

Curious Sea Lions at Tortuga Island **http://www.rtd.com/~bkeller/sharks/slions1.html**
      A diving story.

All links were working at the time of publication but may change; we welcome corrections or suggestions for future editions.